STENCILLING

STENCILLING

Lynne Robinson &
Richard Lowther

Photography by Pia Tryde

Sterling Publishing Co., Inc.
New York

To Robert
who was unable to stay and see this book finished

Art Editor: Alison Fenton
Commissioning Editor: Louise Simpson
Project Editor: Alison Bolus
Production Controller: Mano Mylvaganam
Illustrators: Lynne Robinson and Richard Lowther
Template Illustrators: Chris and Elly King

Library of Congress Cataloging-in-Publication Data Available
10   9   8   7   6   5   4   3   2   1

Published in 2002 by Sterling Publishing Co., Inc.

387 Park Avenue South, New York, NY 10016

First published in 1995 by Conran Octopus Limited

37 Shelton Street, London WC2H 9HN

Distributed in Canada by Sterling Publishing Co.

C/o Manda Group, One Atlantic Avenue, Suite 105

Toronto, Ontario, Canada M6K 3E7

Distributed in Australia by Capricorn Link (Australia) Pty. Ltd.

P.O. Box 704, Windsor, NSW 2756 Australia

Printed in China

Sterling ISBN 0-8069- 6783-8

CONTENTS

Introduction

THE WORD STENCIL derives from old French *enstanceler,* which means to sparkle or cover with stars, and one can imagine the medieval decorator with a fistful of starry stencils and pot of yellow paint creating constellations on a castle ceiling.

Although you will find starry images in our book, it has been our intention to explore the potential of stencilling in contemporary design and decoration and to put a new slant on more traditional designs by alterations of scale and fresh use of color and texture. We hope you will regard the 16 projects we have devised not just as recipes but also as a source of ideas which can be adapted, amalgamated, and added to, so becoming more closely related to ideas of your own.

For us one of the attractions of stencilling is that designs can be produced and reproduced in a controlled manner without any loss of freedom – a reassuring thought for those with little experience. We hope you will recognize its versatility and be more than encouraged to explore the possibilities for yourself.

TOP LEFT *Furniture is a very popular choice for stencilling, though it may not always be done so boldly as we have done here. This imposing screen has a classical appeal and the image has been given texture through the use of sand mixed into emulsion. An Etruscan red wash, sponged off in places, creates highlights.*

TOP RIGHT *Our three cloth projects – a roller blind, a throw and this wardrobe – all use fairly simple images to great effect. Jug shapes and outlines create an unusual blind, while our Tribal Throw design is made from torn-paper stencils and bold paintwork. The wardrobe design is based almost entirely on straight lines, apart from the eye-catching little squiggles on the doors.*

BOTTOM LEFT *Light is an unusual medium for creating a stencil image, but a highly effective one. Cut an image out of opaque plastic film mounted on thick acetate sheet, shine a halogen light through it and create a work of art. Other projects to brighten up interiors include a range of borders, some fake rugs and a full-wall mural.*

BOTTOM RIGHT *Don't be afraid to try out your stencilling skills in the garden too. The Willow Pots we make are much in demand, are not difficult to produce, and they will brighten up a garden at any time of the year. To add further permanent color to your garden, try our Tulip Table or design your own House Sign.*

Tools

MOST OF OUR equipment and tools are not specialist and you will no doubt find many of them around the house. One specialist tool you cannot do without is a scalpel with which to cut the stencil. Our second essential is repositionable spray adhesive, which not only keeps your stencil in place but holds it down flat and so prevents paint seeping under it. Perhaps most important (and cheapest) are a variety of household sponges and a few old white dinner plates, without which we would be lost. The rest you can gather up as and when you need them. Look at our suppliers list on p.94 for suggestions of retail outlets.

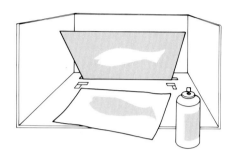

This spray booth is a convenient way to mass-produce designs whilst at the same time protecting your work surface from any excess spray. Registration marks allow for exact placement of the paper to be printed, and the hinged stencil is simply lowered on to the paper and the design sprayed through.

1 Hairdryer. Speeds up paint drying
2 Letter clip. To hang up stencils for storage
3 Repositionable spray adhesive. Indispensable; used primarily to hold stencils in place; unfortunately rather toxic, so use in a well-ventilated room
4 Steel rulers. Better than plastic ones because they can be used as a straight edge with a scalpel
5 Expanding steel ruler. For measuring up larger work
6 Spirit level. For checking horizontal and vertical alignments for work on walls
7 Scissors
8 Eraser
9 Fine lead pencil
10 Water soluble crayon. Can be erased with a wipe of a wet sponge; useful for marking out and making registration marks

11 Artist's sable brush
12 Craft knife. For general use such as cutting cardstock down to size
13/14 Scalpels. Used with a variety of interchangeable blades for cutting stencils
15 Drawing pins. Used to hold fabric in place on a board
16 Latex gloves. To protect hands from toxic and other unpleasant materials such as pigment or cement
17 Cutting mat. Can be used repeatedly without the surface degrading; alternatives include old magazines, some soft linoleum or cork tiles, but they will not last as long
18 Plates. These are our palettes on which we mix large quantities of paint
19 Sponges. Utterly indispensable, they are used in almost all our projects for applying color and texturing paint as

well as mopping up spills
20 Artist's and decorator's bristle brushes. Normally used to mix paint with and occasionally as stencil brushes
21 Decorator's large (10 cm/4 in) brush
22 Hole punchers, eyelet pliers, and eyelets
23 Small dish and real sponges. For finer or small-scale work
24 Storage jar for paint mixtures
25 Steel wool
26 Metal number and letter stencils
27 Small bucket. For larger quantities of paint or water
28 Measuring spoon
29-33 Palette knives, spatulas, and trowels for mixing and spreading thicker media
34 Paint roller
35 Sieve. Can get rid of lumps in paint or large grit out of sand
36 Plastic bowl

Materials

UNLESS YOU AIM to tackle every project in this book you are not going to need everything shown here. Buying a few tubes of paint and some sheets of stencil cardstock will not only get you started but will allow you to cover a lot of ground. We painted a complete wall with such simple means (see p.74). In some projects we mixed other materials into the paint such as sand or whiting to create textures and body or replaced paint with crayons, pastels or even cement mixes. Our list is not prescriptive so don't be afraid to try other materials either by themselves or in combination with others.

1 Three varieties of cement. For making sturdy stencils
2 Rags
3 Kitchen towels
4 Newspapers
5 Zinc phosphate metal primer. For outdoor metal work
6 Acrylic primer. A quick-drying general purpose primer for use indoors or out on wood, plaster, or non-ferrous metals
7 Fine sand. Mixes into paint or cement
8 String. For threading up flags and wall-hangings
9 Sawdust. Gathered from a power sander and used for flocking
10 Tea. Also used for flocking
11 Acrylic gesso. An artist's primer which has a slightly absorbent quality
12 Household emulsion paint
13 Metal leaf. Sometimes known as Dutch metal, and sold in little books
14 Goldsize. For applying metal leaf
15 Conté crayon. A type of hard dry pastel
16 Oil pastel

17 Drawing pen
18 Fixative. For fixing dry pastels, charcoal and pencil drawings, and stencil work
19 Spray paint. An alternative to acrylic paint; gives a flat finish, is quick to use, but it is toxic so follow instructions.
20 Household acrylic paint
21 Whiting. A chalky powder used to give body to emulsion paint
22 White household glue (polyvinyl acetate, or PVA). General purpose adhesive
23 Acrylic modelling paste. One of a variety now available from art stores for smooth, textured, or fancy finish impastos; can be used alone or mixed in with color
24 Acrylic gel medium. Depending on the type this will add gloss, sheen, body, or transparency to acrylic paint
25 Artist's acrylic paint. Widely available, fast-drying paints that come in a large range of colors; the cheaper ranges

are perfectly adequate for most projects in this book but top-quality ones give more colour choice
26 Gilding paste
27 Acetate sheet. Available in various thicknesses; this is a good alternative to stencil cardstock
28 Household white emulsion paint. Provides a good base to work on and can be tinted with acrylic paints; choose thick, good-quality paint
29 A selection of paper bought at art stores and stationers. Used for making cards, wrapping paper, wall-hangings, and flags
30 Lighter fuel. Cleans off spray adhesive and can be used in conjunction with oil pastels to decorative effect
31 Lining paper. For sketching out large designs and for torn-paper stencils
32 Cling film. Used to cover pots and dishes of paint to prevent it drying out
33 Greaseproof paper. Used under fabric and also to store and protect sticky stencils
34 Repositionable adhesive tape. For holding things together temporarily
35 Vinyl parcel tape. For holding things together permanently. Excellent for repairing and joining stencil card
36 Masking tape
37 Stencil card. Available in large sheets from art stores
38 Tracing paper
39 Layout pad. For sketching out ideas, scale drawings, etc. Some contain sheets thin enough to be used as tracing paper

Making and Using Stencils

SIMPLE STENCILS can be engaging in their directness. They also provide the opportunity for you to work fast and thus learn quickly. The tree outline, adapted from a watercolored silhouette, is only one of many simple shapes that could be used. Materials and tools are readily available. You will have to buy a scalpel and some stencil cardstock, but you can also use ordinary cardstock, paper or acetate, or the stencil paper in this book – in fact anything you can cut a hole in. Making the image is a simple procedure. Anything that makes a mark – poster paint, gouache, crayon, pencil, pastels, charcoal, feltmarkers, spray cans – can be used. And although we show here work on paper (and therefore adaptable to wrapping paper, friezes, and greeting cards), the stencils can also be applied directly to walls, doors, floors, fabrics, or wherever you would like them. We are advocating here a free and experimental approach.

YOU WILL NEED

MATERIALS
Paints and drawing media (see left).

TOOLS
Card, paper, and acetate · cutting mat or newspaper · scalpel · repositionable adhesive tape · repositionable spray adhesive · big soft paint brush or stencil brush · sponge · white plate

BELOW *Different treatments of a basic shape (from left to right): gouache dabbed on with scrunched-up tissue paper; oil pastel rubbed in with lighter fuel, additional lines masked out with torn paper; pen and ink; soft pastel rubbed in with fingers; acrylic paint brushed on to cardstock and then transferred through the stencil as a print; rubber masking fluid and gouache; almost dry acrylic paint and a large brush; leaf shape cut into an eraser and printed with acrylic paint; thick oil pastel; oil pastel lines dabbed with lighter fuel.*

1 You can see here a tree cut out of traditional oiled manila card, the translucent paper included in this book, ordinary white cardstock and acetate sheet. All have been cut with a scalpel or craft knife. If using a translucent material, trace one of the trees below. Alternatively, photocopy the image and attach it to the face of the cardstock with a spray of repositionable glue and cut through both the copy and the cardstock. All cutting is done on a cutting mat or a pile of newspapers. Ensure that your blade is very sharp and make the cut firmly and positively, slicing through the material in a single stroke.

2 The stencil can now be used. Attach it to a sheet of paper with repositionable glue or adhesive tape. Paint should not be too liquid or it might seep under the edge of the stencil. Apply tiny amounts with a brush or sponge, building the image up with light dabs until you are satisfied with the resulting texture. Alternatively, use a can of spray paint for quick and even results, or any of the drawing media for varied effects. With such inexpensive means you can experiment and discover for yourself the materials which work best for you.

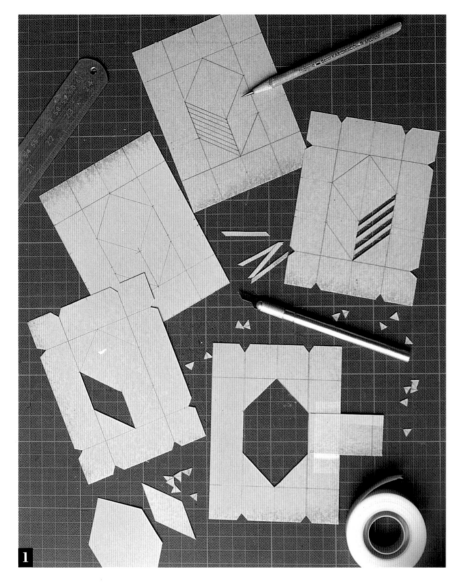

1

Registration

YOU WILL NEED

MATERIALS
Acrylic paint

TOOLS
Pencil · metal rule · set square · stencil card · scalpel · repositionable spray adhesive · repositionable adhesive tape · sponge · mixing dishes

1 If you cut your stencils with care and forethought, you will avoid problems later on. This design is adapted from an axonometric drawing of a cube, which is first drawn on to 5 identical pieces of stencil cardstock. (Although you have only 3 shapes to stencil, as you turn a corner with this particular design you will require mirror images of the stripes and diamond and you will therefore need to cut 5 stencils in all.)

The width of the stencil card must be twice the width of the stencil design. In our example the card is 10 cm/4 in wide and the cube 5 cm/2 in. It has been drawn with precision leaving a margin of 2.5 cm/ 1 in on each side.

We have also left a margin of 2.5 cm/ 1 in at the top and bottom of the stencil. This measurement governs the distance of the design from a feature such as a door frame (as can be seen on p. 65, where a zig-zagging ribbon runs round a door) and so can be altered to suit your own taste. As well as the individual shapes being cut out you can see that notches have been cut in line with the top, bottom, and sides of the motif. In addition, a sixth piece of cardstock is cut into a 5 cm/2 in spacing bar. This is attached with repositionable tape to the edge of the hexagonally-shaped stencil so that it extends by 2.5 cm/1 in (or half the width of your motif) from the edge of the stencil cardstock.

FEW OF OUR DESIGNS require to be positioned with a great deal of accuracy and we often prefer the look of the slight misregister. However, in the example on this page, control is exercised through a combination of accurately-cut stencils, spacing bars, and notches. It is a design suitable for a border and a finished example can be seen on p.65.

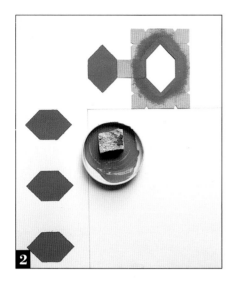

2 In this photograph the pencil line represents the edge of the feature around which you intend the border to go. You can accurately position the first stencil on the corner by placing the bottom edge of the card along this line with the bottom left-hand notch over the corner. Hold the stencil in place with repositionable spray adhesive, then sponge on your acrylic paint.

In order not to risk smudging wet paint by attempting to stencil right next to it, stencil every other motif to start with. Correct spacing is achieved with the spacing bar; because it is attached with repositionable tape it can easily be shifted to the side of the stencil where it will be needed next.

When you start to fill in the gaps you will find that the side notches will line up with the top and bottom points of the motif and so aid in getting it exactly in position and in line.

3 You will now have a line of blue hexagons that will act as the guide for the two remaining colors. Set the edges of the second stencil cardstock along the center of the adjacent hexagons, lining up the side notches with

the top and bottom points of them. As you can see in the picture, the top and bottom notches will be of help as you go around corners. Sponge in your second color along every other hexagon, then fill in the missing hexagons, using the stencil turned through 180° each time to create the attractive zig-zag effect.

Now use your third stencil to create the stripes, again turning it through 180° every time to create the zig-zag. Use the mirror-image versions of the second and third stencils to create the same effect on the vertical runs.

The use of same-size stencil cardstock, notching and spacing bars can be applied to other stencil designs. They not only help in the alignment and registration of repeat patterns and multi-color work, but also allow you to proceed faster when stencilling long runs.

Multi-color Work

THESE ANIMATED geese can be seen on a border in Interior Touches (p.65). Although built up from five stencils, they are not over-complicated to do, though they do require careful alignment. Multi-color work not only allows more complicated imagery to be stencilled but can also introduce a three-dimensional element into the design.

YOU WILL NEED

MATERIALS
Acrylic paint – white, dark gray, Venetian red, black, pale gray

TOOLS
Master drawing · tracing paper · 5 x A4 acetate sheets · scalpel · repositionable adhesive tape · repositionable spray adhesive · sponge · mixing dishes

1 For multi-color work you will need a master drawing that shows in outline all the colored shapes in their correct position, as in our goose template on p.I. You can see here some of the initial sketches for this design and how we separated one goose into 5 colors using tracing paper. You will need to cut a stencil for each color, and the acetate sheets from which they are cut must all be of the same dimension. To position the shapes correctly within the acetate make five A4 photocopies of your master drawing. Place an A4 sheet of acetate exactly over each copy and cut out each color in turn, using your separated drawings for guidance.

Stencils for the body parts have been

designed fairly loosely, but do take extra care with the positioning of the beak, eyes, and feet: a wing slightly out of register will add character to your bird, but a misplaced beak might look rather alarming.

2 Put the first of the stencils in its chosen place and register the location of each corner of the card with 2 pieces of repositionable tape placed in an L-shape. (Use these registration marks to place each of your stencils in turn.) Hold the stencil lightly in place with spray adhesive and sponge in the white paint.

3 Follow the white body shape with the dark gray details, then the Venetian red feet and beaks. While texture can be introduced into sections of the bird's body by sponging them unevenly, make sure that at least the beak is stencilled in flatly and strongly.

4 The fourth stencil is the black neck and body markings, and the final color used is pale gray.

If you wish to make a border out of this image, it will need to be evenly spaced along a line. For this you could

make use of a spacing bar as explained on pp.14-15. Cut this bar to the space required, and tape it to the first stencil. Ensure that it lines up with a positive feature of one of the geese already stencilled, such as the tip of a beak. For closer spacing use the edge of the acetate stencil sheet as a guide, again lining this up with a positive feature on the already stencilled adjacent image. Make a notch in the edge if you find this helps.

Once in position, register the corners with tape and then sponge in each color as before.

PAPER PRINTS

PAPER AND CARD are versatile materials and we have put them to use in making greetings cards, gift boxes and, seen here, festive decorations.

Paper products are easy to obtain – many from local stationery stores, other more unusual ones from specialist paper or art and craft shops. Searching through their shelves of papers is a pleasure in itself and inspirational. The paper chosen for the wall-hanging was one of many beautiful handmade papers we saw which could have been hung on the wall without further adornment. With papers such as these it has been our intention to allow the natural qualities to be as much a part of the work as the stencilled image itself.

Festival Cards and Decorations

THERE ARE OCCASIONS in our lives which involve invitations being sent out or decorations made. Asking friends to a house warming or a barbecue can be made more memorable by making cards yourself or preparing flags or bunting for the day. Your friends will be charmed and cherish the personal effort, and in the weeks to follow you will have, tucked into a corner or pinned to a board, a souvenir of the day. Stencilling is certainly a good way to mass produce such things without the end result looking too mechanical. The designs on the following pages show only some of the many possibilities, and the techniques can readily be adapted to your own ideas. You may also wish to modify designs found elsewhere in this book.

YOU WILL NEED

MATERIALS
A selection of colored cards and papers · acrylic paint – pale gray, burnt sienna, transparent green, transparent brown · white household glue · tea · fine sand · fine sawdust

TOOLS
Scalpel · acetate sheet · repositionable spray adhesive · mixing dishes/saucers · small paint roller · a small natural sponge · artist's bristle brushes · metal letter stencils · motif from p.IV · cardboard box · bowls

Our first stencil was influenced by a Picasso line drawing; you could adapt other artists' work in a similar manner. The leaves and trees make simple yet effective designs, and the flocked letters have the added interest of texture.

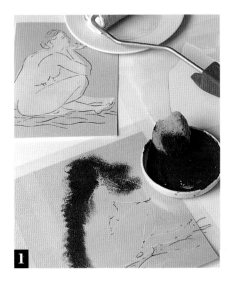

1 If you cut a stencil like this, make sure that the line is broken occasionally rather than a continuous one, to give the stencil some stability. Fine details and crisp edges are more easily achieved with acetate sheet rather than cardstock .

The first stencil is a block of pale gray roughly the same shape as the figure. The color is applied with a small decorator's paint roller. The second stencil is printed on top of the gray in burnt sienna, applied with a natural sponge.

2 The first stencil to be printed is an enlarged leaf and the paint is rollered on. The green we used is a transparent colour and when applied over a strong red, as here, will appear very dark, almost black. Printing over other colors will produce differing effects. The row of smaller leaves, taken from a guide to trees, are made up of two stencils. The shape of the leaf is sponged on in a transparent brown and the veins and stem are in gray.

3 These cards update the flocking technique once used on wallpapers. Rather than use paint, brush on some glue through a metal letter stencil or an acetate one, cut with the swirl design on p.IV. After using the stencil clean it in a bowl of water, and put your card into a small box. Now sprinkle on to the card the flocking of your choice. We have used tea, fine sawdust, and fine sand. When the glue has dried, use a soft brush to dust off the surplus flocking, which can be used on the next card.

YOU WILL NEED

MATERIALS
A selection of colored papers · acrylic paint – black, gray and blue · white household glue · thin doweling or pea sticks · metallic spray paints · string

TOOLS
Stencils from pp.I and II · scalpel · repositionable adhesive tape · scissors · stencil cardstock · small natural sponge · mixing dishes · repositionable spray adhesive · cardboard box

1 The flags have been cut out of colored papers, some of which have a metallic finish. There are two types of flag, a straight one and one cut to look as though it is waving slightly. To sponge the border, you can mask the straight one with tape but you will have to cut a wavy mask to match the other flag. Sponge the border in lightly, leaving it textured. The bandsmen are made up of three stencils (see p.I). They are fairly simple shapes and you should be able to position them accurately enough without recourse to registration marks. Begin with the body shape, sponging it in quite solidly (in this photograph in black), and then the gray details of the suits, and finally the blue of the instruments. Once it is dry, the end can be glued around a stick and it is ready for use.

2 We have designed the flags to be cut out after they have been stencilled. One spray with the metallic paint, gold or silver, will produce six flags, each one different. The stencil, on p.II, has been designed to fit on to paper of A4 size. For mass production we made up a spray booth from a cardboard box and hinged the stencil inside it, as shown in the drawing. The paper to be printed is placed inside the booth, and positioned on registration marks. The stencil is then lowered on to the paper and sprayed in with a color. Each flag is then cut out with a scalpel. To hang the flags, snip off the top corners and fold the end down a few millimeters/ 1/4 in, then glue them at intervals along the string.

BELOW *An alternative design using straight-edged flags alternating with tassels of string knotted between each flag.*

Starry Wrapping Paper

WE HAVE DESIGNED a range of gift wrap, each with its own starry imagery.

Use brown kraft paper as your base or colored versions of this; look out also

for more unusual papers or recycled ones. The stars, freely applied or

organized in constellations, will make your paper sparkle.

YOU WILL NEED

MATERIALS
A variety of papers · acrylic paints – yellow ochre, dark green, pale green, dark blue, pale blue, black, rich red · gold spray paint

TOOLS
Stencils from p.III · scalpel · acetate sheet · repositionable spray adhesive · mixing dishes · small sponges · stencil cardstock · repositionable adhesive tape · scissors · scrap paper · artist's brushes

1 Star shapes are easy to invent or find. We discovered the starfish in a naturalist's guide to the sea shore and printed it in a random manner on blue craft paper using yellow ochre paint. The second star owes a lot to Henri Matisse. It is printed, also at random, in gold spray on to crystal paper. The third star, an eight-pointed one cut with an irregular edge, has been more carefully positioned on the paper. To register this design cut the stencil out with a square border and move it one square at a time as though on an imaginary checker board. Register each move with repositionable tape to give yourself the next position. We chose a mid-green craft paper. Most of the stars are dark green with the occasional pale one for contrast.

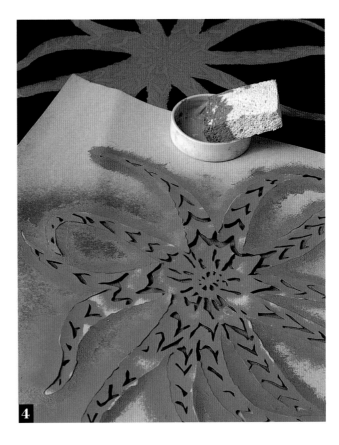

2 We began these papers by cutting scrap paper into strips, spraying them with adhesive and placing them on sheets of colored paper. The uncovered areas were then sponged or brushed over, using an almost dry brush, blue on blue or black on red, and the strips removed to leave stripes. Both stars are two-color and therefore two stencils will have to be cut but they do not require any registration methods. They are printed in two stages, the first being the solid body of the star. The second color is printed on top of it. Slight misalignment will not matter and will probably add to its charm. On one of the papers the stars follow a wavy line cutting across the stripes and they are sponged in ochre and rich red. The stars running along the stripes are first sponged in blue and the second color is a gold spray (see p.23).

3 These three-colored stars, printed on a soft and translucent handmade Japanese paper, have a gentle, organic shape and sparkle with little dots of blue. As they are not symmetrical, we advise you to mark the top and bottom of the stencil with notches to help you line up each stencil the right way round. While precise placement is not too important, do make sure that the outer dots line up with the points.

Begin by sponging in the pale green body of the star and follow this with the gray line around the edge, then finally sponge on the spots. Allow the paint to dry between each stage.

4 Our big starfish requires a lot of cardstock, but to economize we have designed the two stencils to be cut from the same piece. First cut the pattern, the blue parts in our picture, and then cut around the outline of the starfish carefully so as not to damage what you have already cut. Put this to one side and print as many big yellow ochre stars as you wish with the stencil that remains. Now replace the starfish-shaped piece, sealing the cut all around with tape but making sure that you have not covered up the pattern holes. (If this does happen, it is a simple matter to cut these bits away with the scalpel.) You will now have a second stencil ready to use again and you can proceed to print over the yellow ochre in a vibrant pale blue.

Sectional Wall-hanging

SECTIONAL WALL-HANGINGS are versatile objects, adaptable in size and shape to suit most rooms and walls. Not only can you move them from one site to another, you can also shuffle the elements around within the composition for differing effects.

This design is a very simple one of squares and curves, contrasting the natural look of a dense earthy pigment on a rough handmade Indian paper with a vivid blue acrylic paint thickly applied in sweeping arcs across the whole design. To hang it we found a linen twine with a similar natural look to the paper. The geometry of the whole piece is deliberately imprecise as we wanted the end result to be a design that was not too rigid, and had some energy to it. Abstract designs are not the only possibility. An equally good image for this hanging would be the range of leaves seen on our wall mural on p.74.

The work could be hung in other ways and the blue lines scattered across the hanging in unconnected arcs or, as in our photograph, connecting up to form large curves.

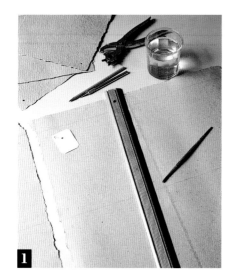

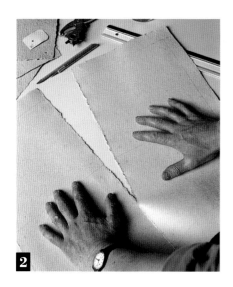

YOU WILL NEED

MATERIALS

5 sheets sturdy textured paper (80 x 50 cm/ 32 x 20 in) · sanguine Conté crayon or pastel · fixative · light blue acrylic paint · acrylic gel medium · metal eyelets · twine

TOOLS

Ruler · pencil · small paintbrush · jar · hole punch · thick stencil cardstock · scalpel · repositionable spray adhesive · eraser · repositionable adhesive tape · palette knife · eyelet pliers · parcel tape

1 Mark out six 24 cm/9 ½ in squares on the back of each sheet of paper. Mark also the position of the holes in each corner of the squares at a point 2 cm/¾ in in from the edges. This can be done with a template to speed things up. To tear the squares in a controlled way, wet each line with water applied with a small brush using a straight edge as a guide. With very thick paper score it gently with the back of the scalpel blade before wetting it.

2 Once wet the paper can be pulled apart along the line leaving a softer edge than if it were cut. On a flat surface, hold one side firmly with the flat of the hand and gently pull the other side out sideways. Punch through the marked corner holes.

4

4 The large curved stencil could be made by tracing off an improvised template, such as a table, or by enlarging a smaller curve on a photocopier.

To mark the position of the blue lines, lay out the hanging on a smooth floor, leaving a 5 cm/2 in gap between each square. Hold the squares in place with tape. Cut the stencil much longer than required and use it initially to mark out each curve a bit at a time in soft pencil. Each section can now be stencilled separately but it may be wise to number them on the back for ease of assembly.

In contrast to the natural look of the pastel on paper, the lines are in a pale blue acrylic paint mixed 50:50 with a gel medium. This mixture is buttered on to the paper with a palette knife. Don't attempt to fill in the stencil completely or make any effort to smooth it out – leave it textured. Where two lines cross, let one dry before painting the second. You can cut the stencil in two if you wish so that it lies flat on either side of the first line. Afterwards the stencil can be made whole again for re-use with strong parcel tape.

Once dry, fit the eyelets. The work is hung by threading the twine vertically through the holes and attaching each vertical set of squares to a picture hook.

3 The stencil needs to be cut from a 25 cm/10 in square of thick cardstock to make it durable enough for repeated use. Cut out the four squares, as shown in the photograph, without the aid of a straight edge to produce a looser shape.

Place the stencil on one square of paper. Don't worry about positioning it too precisely in the center of the paper or too square to the edge: making each one slightly different will impart some movement to the composition as a whole and prevent it from becoming too severe a grid structure.

Color in the squares with the pastel or crayon. This requires some diligent scribbling to build up a thick, textured layer of pigment without any of the paper showing through. Some of the pastel powder will creep under the stencil, resulting in a halo around the image. Leave this as it is. Other unwanted marks and finger prints must be removed with a soft eraser before you fix the pastel with a generous spray of fixative.

FURNITURE FINISHES

AFTER WORKING on paper, we move to stencilling work that is less ephemeral. Well-designed and executed stencils can radically change the look of large pieces of furniture or be employed to decorate small objects such as the stool and tray seen here. Equally, they can be part of the way you paint pictures, and two of our smaller pictures, also in this photograph, are made almost exclusively with stencils found in this book. As a beginner, you may find this size attractive, but don't be afraid to take on larger projects. Those we have chosen for this chapter are not difficult and can be very enjoyable to do.

We hope they will inspire you.

Furniture and other articles of all sizes can be decorated with the
help of stencils and a little knowledge of paint finishes.

Etruscan Screen

OUR FIRST PROJECT could not be much simpler – it involves just one stencil and two colors. The size of the image gives it its dramatic impact and it would work equally well on a door, large cupboard, or wall. We have opted to put it on to a screen. The one used for the project is a metal-framed one, bought new then stripped of paint and allowed to rust before being fitted out with MDF panels. You could, alternatively, use a ready-made screen of MDF or wooden panels, or rescue an old one and put it back into service. The image of an old stoneware oil jar is borrowed from the ancient world. We wanted the texture to mimic old stoneware which has long been buried, and you may be a little surprised to find that this can be done with a mixture of sand and emulsion paint trowelled on and then over-painted. Highlights give the impression of a gentle light falling on the pots.

LEFT *Simple subdued coloring coupled with a gritty texture result in a sophisticated Italianate screen.*

RIGHT *The jar we used will have to be redrawn to fit the dimensions of your screen. Either enlarge our design (or your own) on a photocopier, or sketch it out full size on a large length of paper, such as a wallpaper offcut. For perfect symmetry, first mark a center line and then draw one half of your vase in soft pencil. Fold the drawing outwards along the center line and cut through both halves along the drawn line.*

YOU WILL NEED

MATERIALS
A screen · acrylic primer · red, brown, and white matt emulsion · sand

TOOLS
10 cm/4 in paintbrush · thick acetate sheet (sold by the meter in fabric stores) · scalpel · repositionable spray adhesive · trowel · palette knife · bowl · sponges

1 Coat your screen's panels on both sides with acrylic primer and leave to dry. Mix the Etruscan red, a color that is a feature of Pompeiian wall paintings, from equal quantities of red and brown matt emulsions. Paint both sides of your panels with it and again leave to dry.

Meanwhile, lay your paper cutout on top of the thick acetate sheet and cut out the design with care, saving all the pieces.

Place your first panel on a flat surface and lay the large stencil in position, having first sprayed the back with repositionable adhesive. There are two small pieces of stencil from inside the handles which now need to be correctly placed, and to do this you need to place the jar back into its own shape as a guide. Spray the small pieces with adhesive and pop them into place, then remove the guide with care.

2 Mix 1 part sand into 2-3 parts white emulsion to create a thick, gritty paste. Ensure that your stencil is firmly attached, then proceed to trowel the mixture on to the panel. It need not be very thick. Aim for a rough, textured finish by moving the trowel in all directions, allowing the tool to leave marks on the surface – but beware of overdoing it. Keep the acetate's edge as clean as possible by scraping off the paint and sand mixture with a palette knife. Do this as you proceed with the trowelling since the mixture will begin to set quickly. This will allow you to lift off the stencil easily, leaving a crisp edge. It also makes the stencil easier to use on the next panel.

3 Once it is dry, give the whole panel a generous second coat of the Etruscan red, working it into the texture of the jar with the brush.

4 Three-dimensional form is given to the jar by creating highlights with a wet sponge. Keeping a bowl of water alongside to squeeze out the sponge in, dab away at the jar to spread the color and lift it off along one edge. This should be as subtle and delicate as possible – just enough to create the illusion of vessels barely illuminated in a palace vault.

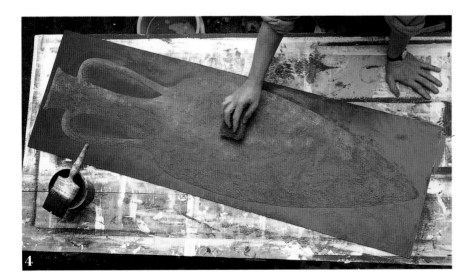

Fishy Kitchen Cupboard

THIS SHOAL OF FISH swimming around a cupboard has been created with just four very simple stencils used many times over. Building up through repetition is a design method not only fundamental to pattern making but also exploited in other areas of design and by some contemporary painters. Stencilling is obviously well suited to this method. The cupboard on which the fish are swimming was a bare wooden one, bought second hand. Our notebooks show that when planning this project we had fish swimming across a screen, as though in a tank. They could equally well be floating across a table top or darting along a wall. Little registration is needed, but you do need to keep an eye on the spacing between the fish. The worn look is accomplished by rubbing back each stage gently with steel wool to reveal a little of what is underneath; the glitter of fish scale is put on in metal leaf.

BELOW Reproduced here full size are the stencils you will need for this project. Stencil 1 is the small fish; stencil 2, a stylized water swirl, is added next. Stencil 3 is the larger fish, and stencil 4 adds the details of eyes, mouth and gills. (Use stencil 3 as a guide for positioning their details accurately.) Use stencil 3 again for the shadows; finally, add gleaming "scales" with metal leaf.

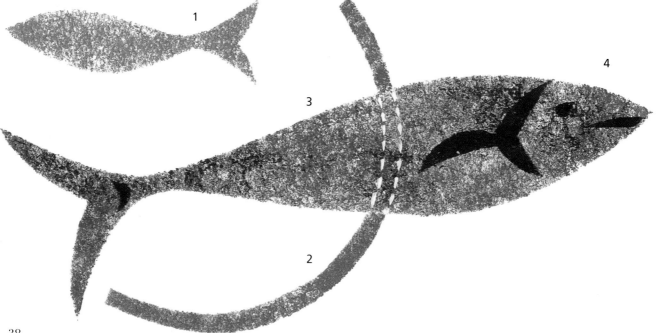

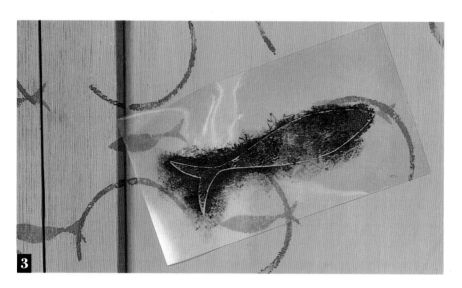

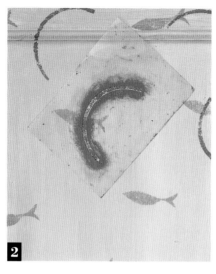

YOU WILL NEED

MATERIALS

A cupboard · undercoat paint · blue topcoat paint · a selection of acrylic paints – cyan blue, navy blue, phthalocyanine green, crimson, paynes gray, white · goldsize · metal leaf

TOOLS

10 cm/4 in paintbrush · fine grade steel wool · acetate sheet · scalpel · soft artist's brushes · repositionable spray adhesive · sponges

1 Choose a cupboard without too deep or complicated moldings, which could hinder the placing of the stencils. If it is an old cupboard like ours it may need a bit of cleaning up first and rubbing down with glass paper.

Begin by painting it with the undercoat and then a top coat of blue paint, which will be the background for your fish. When dry, rub the blue paint back a little with the fine steel wool. Some wood can show through the paint but don't rub too fiercely or you will have little paint left. The first stencil is the smaller of the two fish. Sponged in blue-gray, they are evenly distributed across the front, sides, and top of the cupboard and always swim in the same direction, as shoals do. Sponge these and all of the subsequent stencils lightly, varying the texture within each one. As they dry, rub back lightly with the steel wool.

2 Stencil number 2 is a stylized swirl of water in the form of an arc. Sponge this in a slightly brighter blue-gray and spread the swirls evenly right across the cupboard's surfaces, occasionally crossing a small fish. Give some of these a light rub with steel wool too.

5 To metal leaf the fish's scales, you will first need to apply dabs of a type of varnish called goldsize, and then leave them to go tacky. (The instructions on the jar will tell you how long this is likely to take.) Lay pieces of leaf into place then gently rub them down with a soft brush. The leaf will stick to the goldsize and the surplus can be brushed off.

Real gold leaf is not recommended but cheaper Dutch metal is a good alternative. Other possibilities to consider are gold powders, gold paint, or gilding paste.

The knobs on the cupboard were new ones and these have been given the same paint treatment as the big fish.

3 The second fish (stencil 3) swims in the opposite direction, sometimes in front of, and thus on top of, in painting terms, the little fish. The coloring is a little darker than the small fish, mixed with a touch of green; from time to time a dab of crimson is added with the same sponge. A final stencil (4) is also needed to add the eyes, mouth, and gills, which are sponged in a darker blue or brown. (See the feature details on the larger fish, opposite.)

4 A shadow makes this fish appear to swim in front of the cupboard. Using the same large stencil, carefully put these transparent shadows just below and behind each fish in a thinned-down bluey-gray. Where you wish to position a shadow partly behind a fish, as in the top left-hand corner, use the discarded center of the stencil to mask off the work you have already done.

Bowline Mirror

TO MAKE THE central knot stencil for this mirror, we tied a bowline loop in a length of ribbon and put this on the photocopier. The stencil was then traced directly off the resulting copy. The striped motifs above and on each side of the mirror are all made with one simple stencil. The different shapes result from masking out sections of the design with torn paper and repositionable adhesive tape before putting down the stencil. This technique is one that could be used with a number of stencils giving them greater usefulness and your work more variety. The final stencil of the twigs was based on samples found in our garden.

Before we began on the stencilling, our first task was to cover the bland surface of the MDF with a textured paint finish. You might choose, instead, to look out for a panel which already has an interesting surface to work on. Rusted steel or old floorboards?

LEFT *The mirror surround has been left large, giving us the freedom to decorate it in this style. You can, of course, use a smaller panel or bigger mirror and modify the design accordingly.*
BELOW *The stencilling ideas for this project could be put to use in a variety of ways. The line of twigs also features on our rugs in the next chapter. The knot could wrap around a pot or loop along a wall.*

YOU WILL NEED

MATERIALS
Panel of MDF (medium density fiberboard), 70 cm x 70 cm x 12 mm/ 28 in x 28 in x ½ in · acrylic primer · white emulsion · whiting · acrylic paints – cobalt blue, yellow ochre, burnt sienna, paynes gray, white · mirror tile 15 cm x 15 cm/6 in x 6 in · cement for mirror · D-rings · wire or cord for hanging

TOOLS
5 cm/2 in paintbrush · kitchen bowl · spoon · wooden spatula · 10 cm/4 in paintbrush · metal spatula · palette knife · acetate sheet · scalpel · repositionable spray adhesive · sponges · masking tape · torn paper

1 Prime both sides of your panel, leaving bare a square in the center where the mirror will be glued. There is a risk of it warping if you paint only one side. In the bowl mix some whiting in with the emulsion to make a spreadable paste. With a combination of brush, spatula, and palette knife spread this across the panel and down the edges. The texture can be as wild or as subtle as you wish, according to taste. Allow this to dry thoroughly. It is a thick coat so it may take a day or more.

2 Color this surface with a thin wash of cobalt blue followed by an uneven wash of yellow ochre. The color will run into the hollows and fall away from the high spots, giving more interest to your paint texture.

4 Use the same stencil to fill in between the yellow lines with a pale blue. Since this requires one stripe less, one of the stripes will have to be blocked off with masking tape or a fragment of paper. Once the yellow ochre is dry, reposition the stencil and sponge the cobalt blue into the gaps. Finally, remove the stencil, masking tape and torn paper to reveal stripey shapes produced with the same stencil but in varying shapes.

5 For the final stencil we selected six twig shapes and cut two to each stencil. They are reproduced on p.43, from which you can trace and cut a stencil; alternatively, you can, of course, base your own stencil on twigs you find. Sponge these, using the burnt sienna, in a random order across the bottom of the panel, painting them in quite flat, almost as if they were shadows.

The final task is to glue the mirror into its central space, using special mirror tile cement. Leave it to dry horizontally to ensure that the mirror stays in place. For wall mounting, screw in some picture-hanging D-rings, making sure that your screws are no longer than the thickness of your board.

Trace your stencil of the bowline knot from p.IV, enlarge it and transfer it to the acetate sheet. Position it centrally over the mirror space, then sponge in a cobalt blue and paynes gray mix. Give it texture by pressing down a clean damp sponge on to the paint before it dries.

3 Mark out the inner edges of the stripes with a line of masking tape all around the square. Place another strip about 10 cm/4 in away on either side of the mirror, and ,after pressing it into place, trim a couple of millimeters/ ½ in off each side with a scalpel to give a looser, wavy edge. Tear the paper at random and spray it lightly with adhesive. Then place it in position. Now place the stencil to one side of the mirror space, ensuring that the lines are placed at right angles to the mirror. A line drawn on to the masking tape may help you line up the stencil. Attach it with the adhesive, and sponge over it with a pale yellow ochre. Repeat this for the other side and the top.

CLOTH
WORKS

FABRIC IS very well suited to being decorated through stencilling, be it a stiff lampshade or a soft chair cover. We believe in taking a bold approach to cloth rather than just adding fiddly borders but this does not mean that the work has to be brash or garish. The equipment you will need is the same as for other projects in this book and you do not necessarily have to buy special fabric paint – the majority of our projects are done with acrylic paint. An ability to sew would broaden the range of things you could stencil but even without this skill there are many objects which would benefit from an individual touch.

Our first project, a blind, is one such thing.

Our ideas for the projects in this chapter could be extended to accompanying articles of furniture.

Jug Roller Blind

ON THE DAYS when we have to pull down the blind against the sun's glare, we still enjoy the shadows cast upon it. With this thought in mind we set out to create a design that could give a hint of sun on duller days. Our starting point was a sunny day when we traced off the shadows of three pots and developed them into a simple stencil. As roller blinds are easy to install, this project can be completed in one day. Cans of spray paint speed things up considerably and they produce flat even results without distorting the fabric. You will need to work with plenty of fresh air, however (outside if possible). Alternative designs could be the large leaves from the Leafy Mural or the Sectional Wall-hanging.

Whichever design you choose, you will discover that a design on a blind works in two ways – with the light behind it it's seen in silhouette, but lit from the front the colors come alive.

BELOW *These classical garden ornaments would make an elegant alternative to our jugs. One image used large or repeated, or a selection of shapes would be well suited to a garden room.*

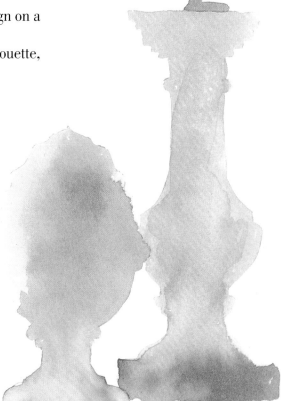

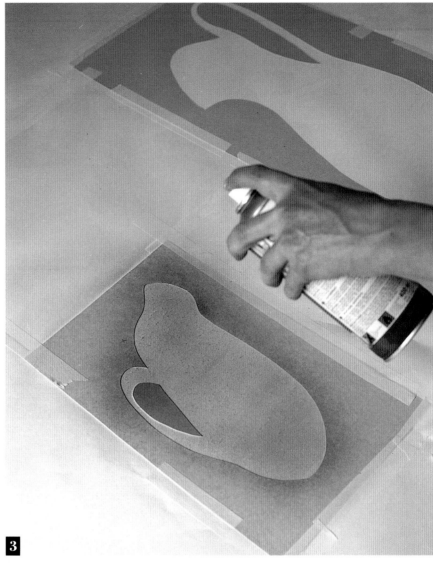

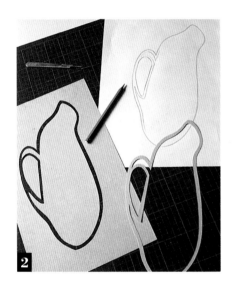

YOU WILL NEED

MATERIALS

A roller blind · metallic spray paint · acrylic paint – yellow ochre, phthalocyanine blue, white

TOOLS

A selection of jugs · drawing paper · matchbox · pencil or pen · ruler · repositionable spray adhesive · stencil cardstock · scalpel · lots of scrap paper · masking tape · sponges

1 Choose a sunny day to start this project. Early morning or late afternoon will give you the longest shadows. Place each jug in turn on the drawing paper, raised up on a matchbox or two in order that you may see the bottom of the shadow that will be cast. Trace with a pencil or pen, as carefully as possible, a line around each shadow. These initial drawings can be enlarged or reduced if need be, so don't worry if you have only small jugs and a large blind, or vice versa.

2 Within this trace you will need to draw an inner line at a distance of 5 -10 mm/¼-⅜ in, depending on the size of the jugs you have chosen. Note that the line meets itself as you come to the handle. Attach the drawing with a light spray of adhesive to a piece of stencil cardstock and cut with care around these two lines. Your stencils will be the inner jug shape, including the space inside the handles, and the outer jug shape.

4 It will not take long to dry so you will be able to proceed quite quickly down the blind.

To make the stencilled lines that echo the shadow shapes, use the same stencils, but with the previously cut-out inner shape of each jug now reinserted. These outlines overlap the shadows at random, changing color as they do so. To accomplish this, first position the pieces of your stencil using spray adhesive. Now mask off with tape those parts of the outline that overlap the shadow shapes. Then sponge the paint, a mixture of blue and white, fairly thickly but not too evenly on to the white background. When this blue line has dried, mask it off in the same manner then sponge in the yellow ochre across the shadow shapes. Although it dries quickly and can be installed almost immediately, leave the blind unrolled for 24 hours to give the paints ample time to set.

4

3 Lay the blind out on a flat surface and roughly plan out where the stencils are to go. They can go off the edges of the blind if you wish. To facilitate this, remove the blind from its pole and slide out the batten from the bottom edge. Starting at the top, lay out the outer stencils of the first three jugs, including the shape inside the handle, using repositionable adhesive to attach them flat to the blind. This is important as we are using spray paint and this will creep under any edge that lifts up. Since it will also spray beyond the stencil's borders, you will have to totally mask out the rest of the blind with scrap paper, securely attached with masking tape. The jug shapes can then be filled in with metallic spray paint. For it to look like a shadow this must be done as evenly as possible so do not hold your can too close to the work.

Tribal Throw

THE CHALLENGE HERE was to make something with the most basic of means. The stencils are made from torn paper and the paint used is household emulsion (vinyl). This may sound primitive but the work is still carefully crafted and the end result in no way reflects the remarkably economical manner in which it was made. We settled on a throw to print our design on, it being an adaptable object able to brighten up a chair, overspread a bed, or mark your space on the beach, and if it gets too cold in any of these places you can wrap it around yourself. The design draws on a variety of sources and influences including tribal patterns, the edges of stacked handmade papers, and old slate walls. The contrasting blue, white, and yellow ochre coloring, deliberately evocative of summer, are a lively and engaging combination. These all come together in two seaside-colored striped bands held in place by thorns.

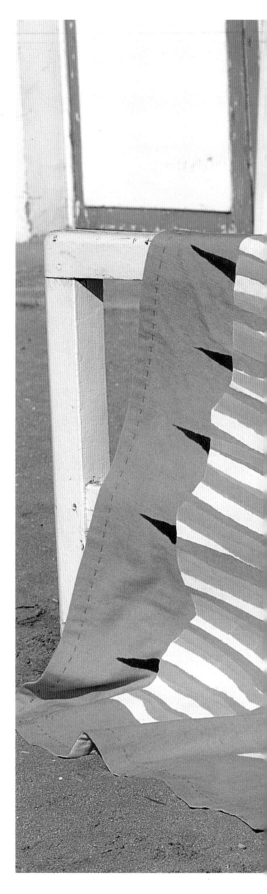

The technique of torn-paper stencils used for this throw could also be applied to deck chairs and windbreaks or in the home on chair covers, cushions, or curtains.

YOU WILL NEED

MATERIALS
Ochre-colored cotton fabric (180 x 140 cm/72 x 56 in, plus extra for testing) · white emulsion (vinyl) · phthalocyanine blue and burnt sienna acrylic paints · cotton lining material

TOOLS
Greaseproof paper · roll of drawing paper · repositionable spray adhesive · 2.5 cm/1 in paintbrush

1 Test a spare piece of the cotton fabric for color fastness and paint absorbency. If paint passes through the cloth you will have to think about protecting the surface on which you are working. Ordinary paper is not very suitable as it will almost certainly become stuck to the fabric, but greaseproof paper is a good solution.

Our stencilling paper is a cheap drawing paper, not unlike newsprint, bought on a roll. Do not be tempted to use newspapers as the spray glue will bring out the ink in it. Tear out the shapes rather than cutting them. This may sound simple, and indeed it is, but it is worth noting that most papers of this type have a grain along which the paper will tear smoothly, and across which the tear lines will be rather more wayward. We have used this here by laying long ragged-edged, i.e. across-grain, tears down the length of the throw to create the edges of the two striped panels.

While it is clear that the measurement will vary, the panels are approximately 30 cm/12 in in width with a similar gap between them. Set uneven stripes down these panels using paper torn along the grain. Use spray adhesive to hold all of this paper in place while you work.

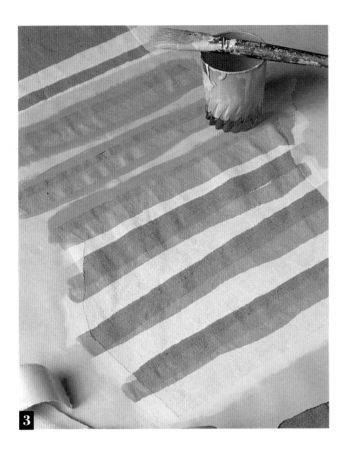

2 Brush white paint into the stripes. We used emulsion on this throw, but you may prefer to test out alternatives such as acrylic paint (with which we have obtained good results) or fabric paint. Whichever you decide to use, test it first for opacity. White pigment will stiffen fabric more than others but it will lose opacity if put on too thinly.

3 When the white emulsion is dry, remove the paper forming the stripes and put down freshly torn strips for the blue stripes. Position these so that the blue line will sometimes overlap the white lines. Where an overlap occurs, a third color will be produced, so again test the opacity of your paint before starting; if it is necessary to thin it down, add no more than a touch of water or it will bleed under the torn paper. Brush on this color, white emulsion tinted with blue, and let it dry.

4 Now remove all of the paper stencils to reveal the two-colored panels. The brown triangular motifs are made in the same manner with three torn pieces of paper for each one. Do not try to make them exactly the same but allow a little variety. They are positioned right on the edges of each panel, not too evenly spaced. Finish off the throw with a cotton lining material (or make two and put them back to back) and it is ready for its first beach, bed, or sofa.

Fairground Wardrobe

THIS WILL SEEM a more ambitious project, but those readers who have a basic knowledge of dressmaking will not have any problems in making this elegant alternative to storing clothes. It is in fact nothing more than a frame with a bag over it, a principle used in tent design. We have used a rudimentary but deep shelving unit bought in kit form comprising four uprights and two shelves. It is deep enough to take clothes hangers, which hang from a sturdy dowel suspended below the top shelf. As a refinement to this rather basic model, we added large industrial castors at the bottom to allow the fabric to hang free of the ground and make it easy to move around. We also trimmed off the top of the uprights to create a completely flat top. A search around local fabric stores should produce something similar that can be covered just as readily as we have this one. The fabric we chose was linen, which is easy to work with and has a classic quality.

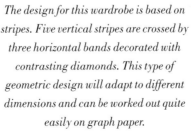
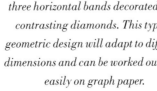

The design for this wardrobe is based on stripes. Five vertical stripes are crossed by three horizontal bands decorated with contrasting diamonds. This type of geometric design will adapt to different dimensions and can be worked out quite easily on graph paper.

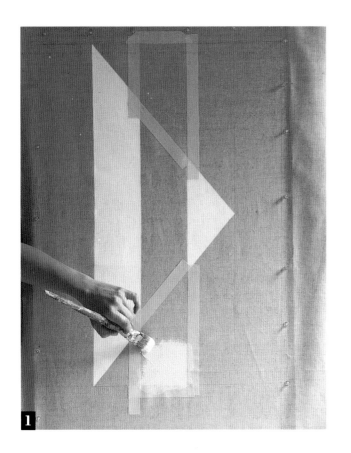

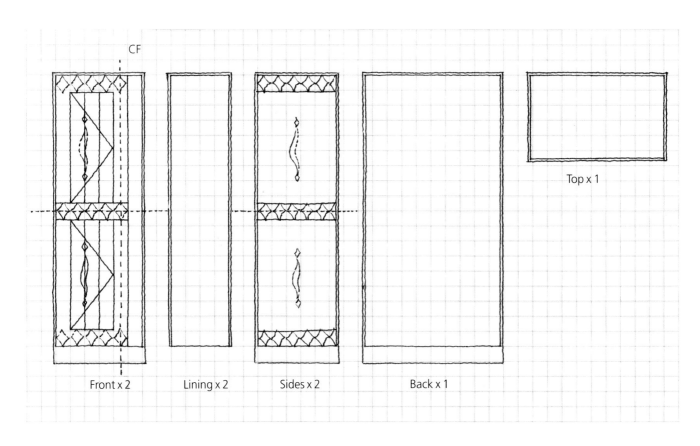

CF

Front x 2

Lining x 2

Sides x 2

Back x 1

Top x 1

YOU WILL NEED

MATERIALS
A deep wooden shelving unit · closely woven, medium weight cotton or linen fabric · cotton lining material · white, green and yellow acrylic paints · cotton thread

TOOLS
Ruler · scissors · tailor's chalk · drawing pins · board · greaseproof paper · artist's bristle brush · masking tape · stencil cardstock · motif from p.IV · pins and sewing needle · sewing machine

1 Measure up your unit, and for ease of fit add 3 cm/1⅛ in to the back width, 1 cm/⅜ in to the front width and 1cm/⅜ in to both the side widths. Add seam allowances, hems, and center fronts (CF) wrap (as shown). These measurements are the basis on which you measure and cut out your fabric, following the instructions in the diagram. The fabric should be preshrunk (wash it if necessary), as the application of paint might cause shrinkage.

Mark the fabric out lightly for painting using tailor's chalk or hard pencil, dividing each front panel into five vertical stripes. The three horizontal bands are equal in width to these stripes plus 20% (in our example the stripes are 10 cm/4 in wide and the bands 12 cm/4¾ in). Mark out the diagonals as on the diagram. On the side panels you need mark out only the horizontal bands.

Drawing pin the fabric panels taughtly to a board for painting. If only a small board is available, you will have to pin it on a section at a time, but unpin it only once the paint is completely dry. Cover this board in greaseproof paper; otherwise ,paint passing through the

cloth will stick to it. Before starting to stencil, test out your paints on fabric off-cuts. Stiffness is not a problem in this project (as it could be for the throw) but absorbency and opacity have to be considered.

Having chosen your paint, and got it to the right consistency, begin with the front panels. Mask out with tape each section to be painted white, in turn. The tape must be very well pressed down otherwise paint will creep under its edges. Apply the paint with a brush, working it into the weave of the cloth. Allow to dry thoroughly, using a hair-dryer to speed things up if necessary.

2 Mask out for the yellow borders, not forgetting that the central horizontal band is in a different color. Brush in the color as you did with the white and then mask out and paint in the central horizontal green band.

3 To locate the position of each diamond, lay a ruler along the edge of each vertical stripe and mark lightly the mid point of the horizontal bands. Cut the diamond motif from card, spray it well with adhesive, and line it up along these points. Sponge the diamonds green on the yellow band and yellow on the green. Place the squiggle and diamond (from p. IV) centrally along the edge of a vertical stripe and sponge in green and yellow.

Apply the three horizontal bands with diamonds, and the squiggle motif in the center, to the wardrobe sides, or altern-atively opt for vertical stripes.

Once the fabric is painted and dry, you can start to assemble the wardrobe. Line the front panels and press each front edge back along the edge of the border. Machine the front panel and lining to the sides along the side border and then machine the sides to the back panel. Pleat

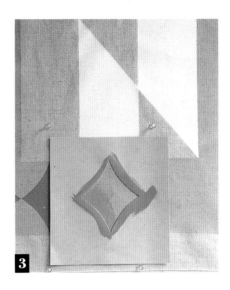

out 2 cm/¾ in at the top center of the back panel, as in a man's shirt, to help prevent the front edges of the wardrobe from pulling open. Overlap the two front edges by the width of the border and, matching corners to seams, machine the front, back, and sides to the top. Hem the bottom edge and press the complete wardrobe carefully, putting a sharp crease down each edge. You are now ready to drop it over the wooden frame. Press drawing pins into the top to adjust its hang and hold it in its final position.

Finally make the ties as shown in the drawing below. Two are positioned on the outer edge to hold the flaps open while the wardrobe is in use. The ties can be placed higher up on the sides if you want to hold them back further. You can now wheel your wardrobe into use.

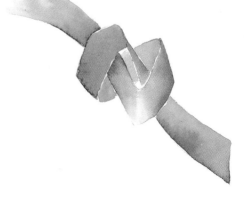

INTERIOR TOUCHES

ONE OF THE big joys and challenges for us when working on interiors can be the scale of the work, opening up the possibility of using large stencils across whole floors and walls, as seen in our Spiral Rugs (p.70) and Leafy Mural (p.74) projects. A certain level of commitment to a big project will be required, as once it is done it will usually be in full view for a long time.

Interior work can also be small-scale, subtle, or even ephemeral. With our lighting project, one flick of the switch and it disappears, leaving just a tantalizing border. Whatever you opt for, you will have something very personal both to you and the room.

Candle light is the surprising media for creating this place name.
Once dinner is over you can blow out the candle
and let your guest go home with a memento of the evening.

Borders

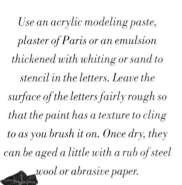

Use an acrylic modeling paste, plaster of Paris or an emulsion thickened with whiting or sand to stencil in the letters. Leave the surface of the letters fairly rough so that the paint has a texture to cling to as you brush it on. Once dry, they can be aged a little with a rub of steel wool or abrasive paper.

WITH A BIT of ingenuity, borders can be made to run around just about any wall, floor, or even ceiling, and any of the motifs seen in this book could be used as a border. Whether they are placed with due regard to a building's features or charge disrespectfully across them, we advocate a boldness in scale. Having said that, the border illustrated on this page is quite subtle and the individual letters on the color-washed wall are about the size of a playing card.

Working upright on a large scale presents certain problems. Use a spirit level when marking out for horizontal borders, attaching string to the wall as a guide for long runs rather than drawing on it, and a plumb line for

vertical ones. However, if your house is old, it may be better to line up borders with existing features. On upright surfaces stencils need to be held securely in place; repositionable spray adhesive is fine for small lightweight ones, but bigger, heavier stencils will also require masking tape. Before drawing pencil guides or sticking anything on to a wall, check first that you can remove it without damage.

Leave internal corners until all other stencilling has been done. Then, rather than bend the stencil card around the corner, slice it in two and stencil each half separately. This may sound a bit drastic but you will be able to tape it back together with parcel tape and use it again. You will even be able to cut it in two again for subsequent corners.

Color washing is a simple technique in which layers of colors are thinly brushed in all directions across a surface. On larger areas use a bigger brush than illustrated.

CUBE AROUND A DOOR

Geometric shapes have an appealing way of joining up with each other to form new configurations and they continue to be central to the work of many artists and designers. This ribbon running around a door is based on an axonometric drawing of a cube and a variation of it can be seen on the Willow Pot on p.80. By reversing alternate stencils, the motifs join up to create a design of two ribbons zig-zagging over each other. Working around interior features such as doors, windows, or chimney breasts will require some initial planning in advance. It is a good idea, for example, to start at the center of the feature and work outward in order to maintain symmetry. Also, make sure the size of the stencil will divide neatly into the length to be stencilled and try a dry run lightly in pencil before committing yourself to paint. A step-by-step guide to this design can be found on pp. 14-15.

SPIRAL

A version of this spiral can be seen on p.70, decorating some rugs. Here we have been quite strict in its alignment and spacing but have turned the spiral a little each time it has been stencilled in order to impart a little movement. Cut the shape out of a circular piece of cardstock, leaving a border the same size as the spacing required between the stencils. You will then be able to proceed quite quickly along a line, positioning the edge of the circular stencil cardstock on the edge of the previously stencilled spiral.

This design would look terrific if used big and stencilled in a pale color on a darker background.

WARDROBE PATTERN

This border design uses an element from the wardrobe on p.56 (the template is on p.IV). A second color has been added, which gives a hint of three dimensions. By alternate turns of the stencil a wave, motion is induced. Unlike the spiral, which exploits a contrast of light and dark, the colors in this design are tonally much closer together.

Simple designs such as this and the spiral are easy to apply and present few problems at corners, doorways, windows, or other obstacles.

GEESE

These geese (see p. I) will require a little more of your time as five stencils are needed plus a sixth for the fence. They are, nevertheless, straightforward, and detailed instructions are given on pp. 16-17. The sample illustrated is quite small, but our tendency would be to make them large, possibly life size, and run them around the bottom of a wall. They do not necessarily have to stay indoors either but could enliven a stretch of wall outside.

LEAFY SWIRLS

This stencil took as its starting point a stylized leaf from an illuminated fifteenth-century choir book. The background is color-washed in parchment shades and then the shadows are stencilled in a darker tone of this color. Note that although only one stencil shape (from p. IV) is required for this border, you will need to cut two of them and use one in reverse.

The impasto effect is achieved with the same acrylic modeling paste we used for the lettering project on p. 62. In this

project some of the paste is colored with acrylic paint before being applied. Use the same stencil as for the shadow, placing it a little above and to one side of it. Spread the paste with a spatula following the curves of the design. Once it is dry you can rub paint or metallic finishes on to the surface. (We have used gilding pastes and stove polishes.) To avoid getting this on to the background, you can mask it off by putting the stencil back into position. The lines running alongside show experiments in colors and finishes for this detail. If the border is positioned along an existing line, a picture rail for example, one or both of these lines may not be required.

FLAGS

You could adapt this design to work well in any room by choosing different colors and finishes. In this example we have sponged on the colors unevenly so that it will not look too static and also give it an air of dappled sunlight. If you do not wish the border to look too freshly painted, a judicious rub with steel wool will give it a suitably older look.

Mask off a strip of wall with masking tape and sponge it lightly in green. Cut the flag shape from the flags as a stencil (the template is on p.II) and sponge it in white on to this green band. On to this white ground, stencil the details in green. You will need to cut two identical stencils and use one in reverse. Use masking tape for the terracotta stripes, and place along them small versions of the diamond from the wardrobe pattern (p.IV). Add smaller flags outside these stripes to the border.

RIGHT *Top left: cube around a door; top center: spiral; top right: wardrobe pattern; center: geese; right: leafy swirls; bottom: flags.*

Lights and Shadows

STENCILLING CAN BE carried out with media other than paint. Looking at sunlight passing through a window and casting an image on the floor led us to explore the possibilities of using light as a medium. We were further encouraged by seeing the signage at the Jeu de Paume galleries in Paris. This lettering, applied to windows and other transparent surfaces, seemed to us like large stencils but in reverse. Sunshine being unpredictable, we turned to artificial lighting and found that the best and most focused shadows were being cast by the outer band of the circle of light thrown by low-voltage tungsten halogen spotlights.

Much influenced by the Parisian gallery lettering, we initially thought of stencilling words with light upon a wall or floor: perhaps "Welcome" on a porch floor or "Happy Birthday" across a wall. Further thought led us to Matisse's illustrations for the book *Jazz*. The original edition of this book was executed in stencils by the publishers Tériade in 1947. Nearly fifty years on these images remain crisp and fresh, and Matisse's technique of cutout paper shapes lends itself well to stencilling. Our own two figures dance with abandon caught permanently in the spotlight. We felt that although they are very striking in their graphic simplicity, they needed a bit of color, so on the wall is stencilled the hooks from which they hang and a fringe of red, all in Matisse's cut-out style.

Try not to draw your figures too stiffly. The dance is more a fling or boogaloo than a minuet, and your drawing style should reflect this. Other images or lettering would work equally well, but don't put in too much detail – go for simple shapes.

YOU WILL NEED

MATERIALS
Clear rigid acetate sheet · black self-adhesive plastic film · low-voltage tungsten halogen spotlight

TOOLS
Drill · black and white inks · drawing paper · tracing paper · artist's brushes · pencil · scalpel · lighter fuel

1 Clear rigid acetate sheeting is available in fabric stores, normally sold as secondary glazing material. An offcut measuring 20 x 15 cm/8 x 6 in is all you will want, and you will need to drill holes in the corners from which to hang it. The black self-adhesive plastic film, intended for use as drawer lining or shelf covering, is also readily available. Peel off its protective backing and press it down firmly on to the acetate. This will be your stencil plate, but make it carefully because it is not discarded afterwards but remains always in view.

Work up your design in black and white ink (either tracing or copying from the pictures of our dancers, or using your own images) and, once you are satisfied, transfer it to tracing paper. This can be done on a photocopier, as in the illustration, or traced in pencil. Attach it to the stencil plate with spray adhesive.

2

2 Remove the sections through which light will pass by cutting through the trace and the film with a scalpel. If you are using a photocopy trace, simply cut out the white sections of your design; if you are working with a line tracing, take great care to cut out the correct pieces. Note also that the acetate sheet scratches easily so cut with care and only on the line. The whole trace and the unwanted parts of the adhesive film will peel away easily and you will be left with your cutouts on the clear acetate background. Any traces of adhesive left clinging to your stencil can simply be cleaned off with lighter fuel.

You will need to explore for yourself the best position for your stencil in relationship to the wall and the light source. Our light is 80 cm/32 in from the wall, and our stencil is hung midway between it and the wall, with the light angled so that the edge of the beam passes through the stencil.

Once it is in position you can stencil colored shapes on to the wall that line up with the cast shadow stencil. These stay in place when the light is turned off and act as a permanent decoration in the room.

Visitors' questions about them can be answered with a flick of the switch.

Spiral Rugs

BARE FLOORBOARDS are an important element of a room, and stencilling allowed us to give ours a decorative treatment that did not hide their character yet made the floor less sparse and more welcoming. Aware that borders around the edge of the room may begin to dictate furniture arrangements, we opted for a less formal all-over design. It is not one that requires a great deal of planning and layout but it will bring a smile to visitors' faces on entering. As you can see, we have scattered fake rugs randomly across the floor. It is an idea that will adapt to any size of room and is quick to do.

The spiral, seen on p.65 as a border design, is a pretty big stencil and we had to make it out of pieces of heavyweight stencil cardstock taped together with parcel tape. It was positioned slightly differently each time so that no two rugs are quite the same. The twigs have already made an appearance on our mirror (p.42) but are used here as part of the decoration and also as fringing.

In contrast to the lighthearted, casual arrangement of the rugs, their coloring is more subdued and classic and will not be an overbearing presence. Elements of the design could be applied to the walls or other furniture. If you wish to continue the playful theme, a real rug could be stencilled in the same pattern and set among the false ones to increase the delight of visitors.

Altering the position of the spiral each time you stencil it will impart movement to the series of rugs.

71

YOU WILL NEED

MATERIALS

White emulsion · raw umber acrylic paint · matt floor varnish

TOOLS

2 large sheets of stencil cardstock · parcel tape · scalpel · newspapers · mixing dishes · paint roller · repositionable spray adhesive · sponges · acetate sheet

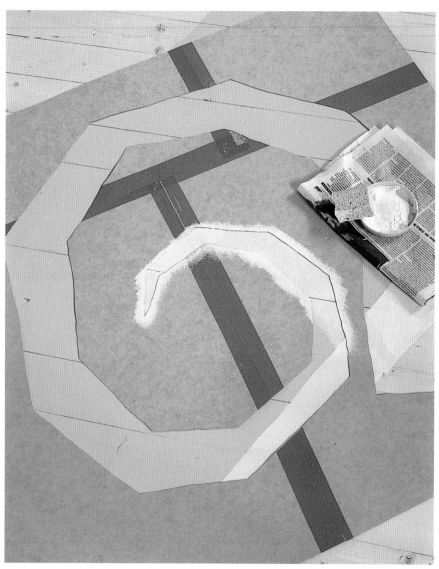

1 Cut strips of stencil cardstock 10 cm/4 in wide and tape them together edge to edge to form a 60 x 90 cm/24 x 36 in rectangular stencil frame. Cut them freehand with an irregular edge to imitate a rug. Make a rough plan of where you are going to place your rugs by laying out sheets of newspaper on the floor, and mix up enough paint (white plus a small amount of raw umber) for all of them. 1 litre/1¾ pints would be enough for up to 18 rugs. Apply the paint with a paint roller for a quick and even finish.

2 While this is drying, tape together large pieces of stencil cardstock and from this cut out the spiral motif (traced from the image supplied on p. 71 and enlarged to your required size). As this stencil will be bigger than the rug outline, you will have to mask off with paper the sections of the floor that show through the stencil. This will vary for each one since the spiral is positioned differently on each rug. Use spray adhesive to hold both paper and stencil in place while you sponge in the white emulsion, using 2 or 3 coats to give a strong opaque white. Use

as thick an emulsion as you can find. (Thin ones require more coats and will seep under the stencil.) An artist's white acrylic paint might be more solid, and therefore easier to use, but it is also rather more expensive.

3 The twig decoration is positioned parallel to one of the longer sides of the rug, but not always in the same place. Cut out of acetate sheet a stencil of about a dozen twigs, in line, based on those on p. 43. Cut the fringing stencil in the same way, using the design shown here. (Being a bit thinner than cardstock, acetate sheet gives a more precise edge to your print, and is therefore good for detailed work such as this.) Sponge the twigs then the twiggy fringing in a similar mixture of white and raw umber, but this time add more of the latter to make the color much darker.

The whole of the floor will, of course, need to be protected with floor varnish. Choose one as matt as possible and try to have the patience to let the paint really dry and set hard before applying it – around 2 weeks.

Leafy Mural

THE INTENTION OF this project was to cover a wall completely, just as fresco painters have since the time of Pompeii. In our own era the American artist Sol Lewitt, whose influence will be found in the structure of this design, has dramatically transformed rooms with his large wall drawings.

The size and position of the grid will need a certain amount of planning in advance on a scale drawing. You would be extremely lucky to have a perfectly square wall into which will neatly fit a grid of this size. We ensured that the design fitted top to bottom and was symmetrical around a door (not seen in this photograph). The design was then allowed to run off at either end. If your house is an old one with walls and corners that are not quite straight and true, take this into account when planning your mural. Try also to plan so that light switches and electrical sockets are within the rectangles rather than on the yellow ochre bands.

We worked with nine leaf shapes, mixing specimens from maidenhair, butcher's broom, and tulip tree with more common shapes such as the oak and laburnum. Ours were traced from a guide to trees, but some readers may like to enlarge leaves from plants in their own gardens. And we mean *enlarge*. These are big stencils cut from more than one piece of cardstock. We mixed up seven colors in advance and this meant we never had to repeat a color and shape combination.

YOU WILL NEED

MATERIALS
Satin finish white emulsion · large tubes artist's acrylic paints – yellow ochre, pale blue, dark blue, pale gray-green, olive green, terracotta, and burnt sienna

TOOLS
Paint roller · tape measure · pencil · long straight edge · masking tape · sponges · mixing dishes · jam jars · motifs from p. V · stencil cardstock · scalpel · parcel tape · repositionable spray adhesive

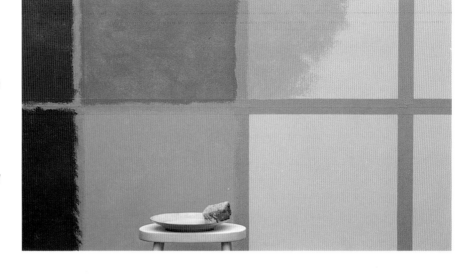

1 The surface of the wall must be sound. Apply two coats of white emulsion (using a paint roller to ensure an even texture) and allow it to dry. The masking tape you use in the first two steps will be easier to remove from a satin finish.

Measure and mark out the grid. The dimensions will depend on the size of your wall and the positions of doors, sockets, light switches, and so forth. As a guide our rectangles are 46 x 48 cm/18 x 19 in, separated by 5 cm/2 in yellow ochre bands. Mask out the rectangles and sponge in the bands with yellow ochre acrylic paint. Gently remove the tape and allow the paint to dry thoroughly before you mask out the bands for the colored rectangles. Take care in positioning the tape exactly along the lines and in forming square corners, and don't stick the tape down too soon or too firmly on to fresh paint as it may damage it on removal. Plan it so that adjacent colors are never the same, and make sure you have enough of each color to complete the wall. (For a wall this size – 2 x 4 m/6 ft 6 in x 13 ft – we mixed up a jam jar full of each color.) Sponge the colors on (you will notice in the illustration that this is done unevenly, leaving a textured surface).

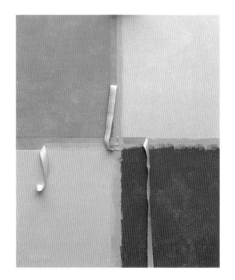

2 Remove the masking tape as soon as possible but be gentle, peeling it back evenly and slowly. You will reveal your multi-colored grid that is now ready to receive the stencilled leaves, drawings of which are reproduced on p. V.

3 To make stencils as large as this, you will need to join together two pieces of cardstock with parcel tape. Don't overlap them but place them edge to edge and tape both sides before cutting out the design. Hold the stencils flat against the wall with spray adhesive, but use masking tape for additional support because they are fairly heavy. Give some leaves, such as this oriental plane, just one coat of paint, using the sponge to build up a texture.

4 Give some other leaves, such as the laburnum seen here, a second color, lightly sponged over the first. This technique extends the color range and introduces more texture into the design. Vary the positioning of the stencils, placing some upright while turning others at an angle or upside down. Where a stalk creeps out of the edge of its rectangle, use masking tape to fill in that part of the stencil temporarily, as demonstrated in the photograph.

Being three-dimensional, electrical sockets are almost impossible to stencil over, and we felt there was little point in attempting to hide them anyway and so left them pristine. Removing them from the wall is easier than working around them, but do switch off the power at the mains first.

After undertaking all this work it would not be right to hide your endeavours, so introduce only a minimal amount of furniture to set it off, as we did for the photograph.

GARDEN
COLORS

FOR THIS CHAPTER we look at the possibilities of using stencilling outdoors, initially taking advantage of acrylic paint's hard-wearing qualities. Ordinary garden pots are the subject of one of the projects and a group of them can have great impact on a terrace. Any plant container could benefit from a face-lift, as would garden furniture such as our small table. Glancing back to the last chapter you might also recognize the potential of some of the border patterns for outside walls or fencing. The third project – a house tile with a raised design – is a more adventurous undertaking in that it uses cement as a medium.

Autumn provides plenty of beautiful colors, but there is no reason why you shouldn't add some of your own that will see you through the year.

Willow Pot

WE HAVE BEEN painting garden pots for a long time now, the first ones being made for friends as gifts. Thus began a minor industry in our studio. They continue to be well received as presents so we can recommend them as potential gifts or as home decoration. Some are hand painted and others are stencilled or are a mixture of the two techniques.

Many of the designs seen elsewhere in this book could be applied to a pot, often with little or no adaptation. Imagine a pot covered with fish, for example, or the abstract imagery used on flags. Or take the knot used to decorate our mirror. All of these and many others could be applied to a pot. Just ensure that your stencil cardstock is flexible enough and that the design is not too big; otherwise, it will disappear round the curve.

The source of the main image for the project on the next page is a stylized willow branch, which was originally part of a decoration in a medieval church. Should you want to use them as plant pots, don't be afraid to put dirt directly in them. We have been testing out the survival rate of the coat of paint and can report that it is holding up well. If the paint has been affected by dampness we think it even adds to the patina rather than detracting from it. If you don't want to plant directly into the pots, an option is to use plastic pots inside the terracotta ones.

LEFT *The 3 stencils which make up the cube pattern around the base are very similar to the ones shown as a border on p. 65. Because you are working on a curved surface, you will have to watch the spacing more carefully and always line the stencils up with the base of the pot.* ABOVE *Trace this drawing of the stylized willow branch to make your stencils.*

YOU WILL NEED

MATERIALS
*A terracotta pot about 30 cm/12 in high ·
white acrylic primer · acrylic paint –
white, phthalocyanine green,
ultramarine, raw umber, cadmium red,
yellow ochre*

TOOLS
*Brushes · dishes · a bowl · sponges ·
paper · repositionable spray adhesive ·
tracing paper · stencil cardstock ·
masking tape · scalpel · water-soluble*

crayon

1 The pot will need 2 or 3 coats of
primer to begin with. Terracotta is
very absorbent, so the first coat must be
diluted with water and applied to a damp
pot to ensure good adhesion.

The first color is a mix of green and
white paint brushed quite liberally on to
the pot, and the patina is achieved with a
wet sponge and lots of water. With the
pot held at an angle, squeeze water out of
the sponge; it will run down the pot and
around it as you turn it. As you dab at
these runs with the sponge, the paint will

be lifted off and surrounding areas will
become textured. This process can be
repeated a number of times. Differences in
the texture will result as the paint dries.
Experiment too with very wet or very dry
sponges. If the result is not pleasing to you
wipe the whole pot clean and start again.

2 The first stencil is simply a torn piece
of paper wrapped around the pot
and held in place with a spray of glue.
Sponge ultramarine on quite strongly
along the edge of the stencil, fading it out
as it goes up the pot.

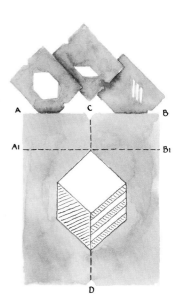

3 The willow branch, shown on p.81, is a three-part stencil. Begin with the stem, sponging in lightly a color mix of cadmium red and raw umber. Next apply the upper section of the leaves using phthalocyanine green. As you can see in the photograph, the third, straight, section has more leaves than is necessary, which allows you to use it in different positions or on larger pots. Mask off with tape the sections not required before lightly glueing it to the pot. As you remove the stencils from each section, press a clean wet sponge to the paint to texture it lightly.

4 Cut each of the stencils that form the line of cubes out of a rectangle of cardstock exactly twice the width of the cube (see drawing, right). Cut notches as shown. Invert your pot, select a starting point, and align the stencil's top edge with the base of the pot (see photograph) and hold it in place with the glue. To place the cubes at the bottom of the pot, use the side notches marked A1-B1 on the drawing. With the crayon, mark on the pot points B, C and D, then lightly sponge in the yellow ochre. Working from left to right, reposition your stencil to the next

space but one along by lining up notch A with the mark previously made at B. Mark out at each notch as before and sponge in the color. Continue around the pot. Once the paint has dried, you can complete the intervening spaces using the existing marks to position the stencil.

Use the same marks to align the final two stencils. The colors of these are the deep red of the willow stem for the solid color and an ultramarine and white mixture for the stripes. Finally, add a little more red to the willow stem color, and then paint the inside of the pot.

Tulip Table

THIS PROJECT aims to take a small garden table, personalize it, and make it special. Ours is a little round metal one bought very cheaply from a garden shop, but you could use one that is larger or square or one made from wood. The stencil can be adapted either by altering the size or by making simple changes in design. The illustrations on this page show just some of the possibilities for larger, square and rectangular tables.

The flower stencil was developed from a watercolor of a parrot tulip and can be used as often as you wish, depending on the size of your table or individual whim. The motif at the center is a circular development of the borders of the patchwork flags of the Fanti people of Ghana – wonderful textiles which have often been an influence in our work. The complete design, or sections of it, can not only be adapted to fit a variety of tables but could be put into service on walls, floors or fabrics.

ABOVE *If your table is larger than ours (55 cm/21¾ in diam.) the design can be adapted to fit. The border pattern could be enlarged, for example, leaving the rest of the design small scale but placing the tulips near to the perimeter. Alternatively, mark out a 55 cm/21¾ in diameter circle and apply the design as a central image with a tulip or two outside it if the table is big.* RIGHT *Illustrated is a way of modifying the design to fit a rectangle. A larger square table could have the design applied 4 times with interlinking borders.*

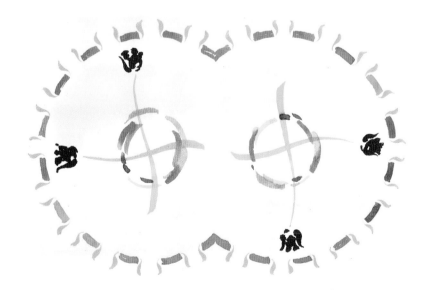

YOU WILL NEED

MATERIALS
Garden table · metal or wood primer (if needed) · acrylic gesso or other artist's white primer · artist's acrylic paint – olive green, cerulean blue, cadmium red, yellow ochre, paynes gray, raw umber, white

TOOLS
Abrasive paper · white plate · brushes (for color mixing) · sponges · bucket · scalpel · stencil cardstock · repositionable spray adhesive · water soluble crayon

1 If your table is bare and unpainted, it will need a coat of primer paint. If you do this well your table will survive for longer outdoors. For metal, a zinc phosphate primer would do the job. (The primer used on cars would probably do just as well, although we have not experimented with that yet.) There is a wider choice of wood primers available; select one suitable for use under water-based paints. Rub down the surface of your table with abrasive paper and dust off before painting. To avoid brush marks, dab it on with a rag or sponge or use a roller. A previously painted table may only need to be rubbed down with abrasive paper and any breaks in the surface touched up with primer. Once dry, give the surface 2 coats of artist's white acrylic primer. We have used acrylic gesso as we like its absorbency, but do not confuse this with real gesso. At this stage texture can be introduced by applying the primer with a sponge or rag.

2 For the first color we sponged on an olive green and white mix with some dabs of yellow ochre. One sponge holds the paint and a second is clean and damp. Use the two in combination to apply paint and lift it off, squeezing them clean in water as you proceed. The paint will dry quickly and as it does the varied texture will be created. Spots can be formed by splashing water on to the surface, leaving them for a few moments and then sponging them off. If you have applied too much paint, press down hard with the damp sponge to lift off the paint.

3

4

3 Make a border stencil of 4 evenly-spaced rectangular sections, which will be repeated to give 16 rectangles in all. Cut side notches and use these to position the stencil accurately and form a circle concentric to the table's edge. (If you are working on a square table or wish to place the design in the middle of a larger round table, you will then need to mark out a circle and line up the notches to that.) It would be wise to do a dry run with your stencil, marking it out with a water soluble pencil in order to spot any inconsistencies in the spacing and making adjustments if necessary. Any pencil marks you make can be wiped off later with a damp sponge.

Once confident that all is well, lightly spray the back of the stencil with repositionable adhesive and press it in position. Mix up a deep blue with the cerulean blue and the paynes gray. Using a damp sponge, apply the paint to the table with a light dabbing action. If you are too heavy-handed paint will be forced under the stencil and spoil the outline. Work up the 4 rectangles quickly, remove the stencil, and immediately press a clean wet sponge on to each section. This picks up some of the paint, leaving it with a texture

similar to, and blending in with, the green base coat. Take care to press or dab with the sponge rather than wipe. Complete the circle in the same manner.

4 Enlarge the central stencil design on p. VI, following the instructions; transfer it on to stencil cardstock then cut out the relevant parts. Take note of the hole cut in the center of the stencil which allows you to position and reposition it accurately over the center of your table. The colors are yellow ochre, cadmium red mixed with raw umber, and the blue of the

border. Spray the back of the stencil lightly with adhesive and decide on your first position. Apply the color as before with a light dabbing action. Which segment you dab it through is not too important, but do use all 3 colors each time you position the stencil. Give attention to the quality of the texture, fading it out along the long stripes by using an almost dry sponge and putting a thin layer on only when you want a color below to show through. Repeat this 2 or 3 times, turning the stencil and aligning it with previously painted sections.

5 The tulip head is a two-part stencil (see p. VI). It must be cut well using the same size cardstock for each part and in the same position on the cardstock (see pp.14-17 for advice on aligning and registering stencils). In this instance we are using the top corners of the border motif to register the tulip, as can be seen. Attach the stencils using spray adhesive. The base color of the flower is cadmium red. If your paint is a bit thin or rather transparent, allow the first coat to dry and apply a second one. This can be done fairly speedily. The shadow details are in a mix of cadmium red and raw umber.

The stem (also on p. VI) is not so much dabbed in with the sponge as wiped down its length, using a green mixed from cerulean blue and yellow ochre and darkened with a touch of paynes gray. Where it passes over the central motif, it can be made to appear to pass below it by taping over that part of the stencil.

6 Finally, add the little blue flicks (a mixture of blue with white). They sit between the dark blue rectangles and just touch the edge of the table. The notches are cut as in the first stencil to line up on the table's edge. They are small enough to be centered by eye between the rectangles and a slight waywardness in their positioning is to be encouraged: it all adds to the charm of a handmade piece.

The table can go in to use immediately and will wipe clean (but don't use abrasive cleaners). It will survive outdoors during the summer and take hot drinks on chilly evenings. Should you wish to give it further protection, you could add a coat of clear varnish: choose matt not gloss. Wait at least 2 weeks before doing so in order to allow the paint to dry out fully and harden off. An unvarnished table will wear a little over time, but we think this also adds to the charm.

House Sign

You won't be able to get rainbow colors in cement, although some brightness can be achieved with white Portland cement as a base. Stick to simple shapes like this tree (above) and star (right).

HAVING USED TEXTURED mixes in earlier projects (the wall-hanging, the screen, two of the borders) we began to experiment with more durable materials for use outdoors, one of which was cement. To extend the range of colors, add dry pigments or stir in a small amount of acrylic paint – not too much though as it will affect the setting of the cement and probably look garish and unnatural. You will have to add aggregates to give strength and durability to a cement mixture. These can be fine or coarse according to the effect you wish to achieve. The most common are sand, gravel, or crushed stone but you may be lucky and find marble chippings or granite. For this project we opted to make a house number but it could also be a house name or an image to set into a floor or wall.

Working on outdoor projects opens up all sorts of possibilities, not only with fresh materials but also with scale. If you can make a cement tile, there is no reason why you cannot go on to make a complete terrace or garden path, or to make a variety of tiles to set into an outside wall. You need not limit your endeavours to your home since we have found that a personalized house sign makes an excellent gift.

wooden board that has been waxed. The wax will act as a glue holding the stencil in place.

Mix 1 part white cement to 2 parts fine sand. (The setting time can be speeded up by using a small amount of quick setting cement, which will make it much more gray-beige in color.) Mix this to a stiff paste with a little water and gently butter it into the stencil with the spatula.

2 The tree must not dry out before the next layer of cement is added, so peel away the stencil almost immediately. If your cement mix is fairly stiff the edge of the image will stay crisp.

3 Position your wooden square around the tree and hold it in place with masking tape. Make up your next layer of cement from 1 part ciment fondu to 3 parts coarse sand to give a gritty contrast to the smoother mix used for the tree. This mixture is gray-black and we have darkened it further with a touch of black pigment. Use very little water in order to create a dryish mix and then delicately spread it on and around the tree. If the mix is stiff enough, it will not seep out under the wood.

YOU WILL NEED

MATERIALS

White Portland cement · quick set cement · ciment fondu · fine sand (sieved) · coarse sand · black pigment · white household glue · red pigment

TOOLS

Rubber gloves · template on p.IV · acetate sheet · scalpel · wooden board · wax polish · bowl · fine sieve · trowel · flexible spatula · 4 pieces of wood, 25 x 2.5 x 5 cm/10 x 1 x 2 in, screwed

together to make a 20 cm/8 in square · screwdriver · screws · masking tape · wood off-cut · damp rags · stiff brush · metal number stencils · pencil · bradawl · artist's paintbrush

1 First, it would be wise to protect your hands with rubber gloves, especially if you have sensitive skin. We begin in an upside-down sort of way by stencilling the tree and then filling in the background from behind. Trace the tree motif from p.IV, and cut a stencil of this from acetate sheet, then press this down on to a

4 Initially, you will have had to spoon in the mix carefully in order not to disturb the tree, leave air bubbles, or move the wooden former. Once you have covered the tree, however, you can fill up the wooden former and tap it down level with an offcut of wood. Ciment fondu will set quickly but it must also be allowed to cure. This will not happen if it dries too quickly so you must now cover the work with damp rags for 24 hours before proceeding to the next step.

5 Lift the tile off the board, unscrew, and remove the wooden former and turn the tile face up. Use a stiff brush to clean the surface and reveal the texture of the darker cement. Using the metal stencils, mark out the position of the numbers and trace their shape in pencil. To ensure good adhesion of the cement numbers to the tile, scratch the surface within this trace with a sharp-pointed tool, such as a bradawl, and then paint the area with glue.

Mix a very small amount of Portland cement as in step 1, color it with a tiny amount of red pigment, and spread it into the metal stencil with a flexible spatula. Don't spread it on too thickly, but leave the tool marks showing. Carefully remove the stencil so as not to damage the edge of the number and leave the cement to set. It should not be allowed to dry out too quickly, so again cover with a wet rag while the cement cures. We imagined the tile set into a wall, but it could have holes drilled into it and be screwed to a wall, or a loop of wire could be pushed into the wet cement at the end of step 4 and the tile hung from this.

Suppliers

Most of the tools and materials you will need for stencilling will be available from local shops: art shops generally stock basic equipment, such as stencil board, acetate sheet, cutting mats, brushes, and paints. Hardware shops are excellent for such items as paintbrushes, varnishes, masking tape, sandpaper, etc. The suppliers listed below are for any more specialist materials you might want.

US

Stencilers Emporium
PO Box 536
Twinsburg OH 44087
216 425 1766

Stencil Ease
Box 1127
Old Saybrook CT 06475
203 395 0150

American Traditional Stencils
Bow Street RD 281
Northwood NH 03261
603 942 8100

American Home Stencils
10007 South 76th Street
Franklin WI 53132
414 425 5381

The Itinerant Stenciller
11030 173rd Street SE
Renton WA 98059
206 226 0306

SOUTH AFRICA

Art and Graphics Supplies
169 Oxford Road
(Nedbank Centre entrance)
7B Mutual Square
Rosebank
Johannesburg
011 442 9563

X-Press Graph-X
29 Siemert Road
Doornfontein
011 402 4522

Crafty Supplies
32 Main Road
Claremont
Cape
021 610 286

AUSTRALIA

Janet's Art Books Pty Ltd
143 Victoria Avenue
Chatswood NSW 2067

Handworks Supplies
121 Commercial Road
South Yarra VIC 3141
03 820 8399

NEW ZEALAND

Homeworks
381 Parnell Road
Parnell
Auckland
366 6119

Which Craft Ltd
288 High Street
Lower Hutt
Wellington
566 1773

Hands Ashford NZ Ltd
5 Normans Road
Papni
Christchurch
355 9099

Acknowledgments

A big thank you to Louise Simpson for having the confidence in us and all the calm support she gave to the project;
to Alison Fenton for infinite patience and splendid design; to Pia Tryde for infectious enthusiasm and brilliant
photography and to Alison Bolus for stoic work on the text.

We would also like to thank Michel and Fabianne Brainin of Honfleur and Alain Forget of Tourgeville for generously
allowing us to use their galleries as locations and a very special thanks to Jean-Claude Herrault of Honfleur who not
only gave us free access to his superb garden and flower shop but also lent us numerous props including
the little *marie* that opens up Paper Prints.

Thanks too to Ratton and Marine, two friends who helped in the realization of some of our projects.

Index

Bandsmen (p. 22) Three stencils are required to make this image. The first is for the figures of the bandsmen, the second for the details of their suits, and finally the third for the musical instruments.

Geese (pp. 16-17) This is a master drawing from which you will have to trace the five stencils needed to make the design. As explained in the text, this task is made simpler if you work from five photocopies.

Bandsmen (p. 22) Three stencils are required to make this image. The first is for the figures of the bandsmen, the second for the details of their suits, and finally the third for the musical instruments.

Geese (pp. 16-17) This is a master drawing from which you will have to trace the five stencils needed to make the design. As explained in the text, this task is made simpler if you work from free photocopies.

Right. The simple tree shape is cut out of acetate and used to make the cement tile on pp. 92-3. We also produced an alternative design featuring a star as seen on p.91. If you wish to choose an image of your own, keep it simple as cement is not as fine a medium as paint.

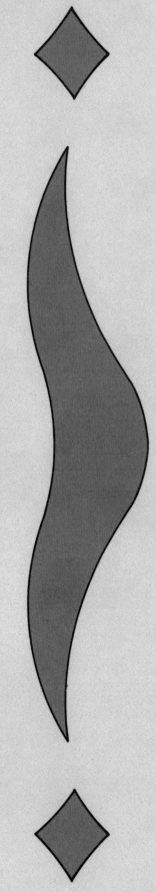

Right. The squiggle and diamond motif from the wardrobe (p. 57.) You will have to enlarge it. Although you will be using two colors with this stencil, cut it as one in order to ensure that the diamonds line up well. The larger the diamonds, which run in bands across the wardrobe, can also be taken from this drawing.

Left. The bowline knot, used in conjunction with twigs and torn-paper stencils for the mirror on p. 42.

Right. The leafy swirl that can be seen on one of the borders on p. 65. Enlarge it to the size you want and cut two of them, using one in reverse to make the pattern.

Right. The simple tree shape is cut out of acetate and used to make the cement tile on pp. 92–3. We also produced an alternative design featuring a star as seen on p.91. If you wish to choose an image of your own, keep it simple as cement is not as free a medium as paint.

Right. The squiggle and diamond motif from the wardrobe (p. 57.) You will have to enlarge it. Although you will be using two colors with this stencil, cut it as one in order to ensure that the diamonds line up well. The larger the diamonds, which run in bands across the wardrobe, can also be taken from this drawing.

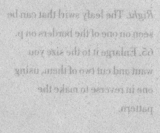

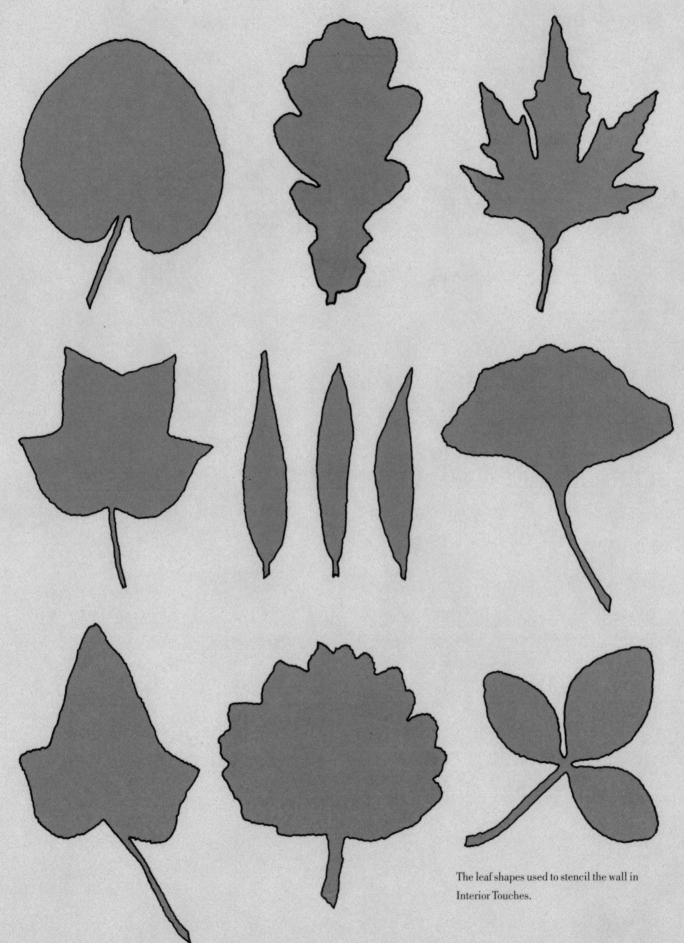

The leaf shapes used to stencil the wall in Interior Touches.

Tulip Table stencils (pp. 86-9) The tulip head is in two parts, here drawn overlapping. The shaded area is for the stencil of the shadows. Mark them out on identical squares of stencil cardstock so that one stencil has those areas not shaded, and the other has only the shaded areas. Ensure that the two parts register perfectly before you cut them out.

The stem can in fact be to the length and curvature of your choice. Otherwise, enlarge this drawing and trace off on to stencil cardstock.

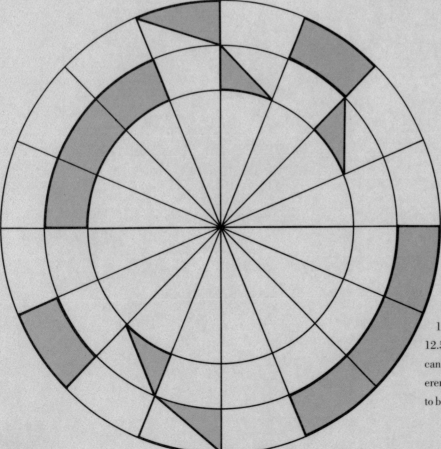

Enlarge the design for the central motif shown here so that the outer circle measures 21 cm/8¼ in, the middle one 17 cm/6¾ in, and the inner one 12.5 cm/5 in. The size of the circle can, of course, be altered to suit different circumstances. The sections to be cut out are shown shaded.

Tulip Table stencils (pp. 86–9) The tulip head is in two parts, here drawn overlapping. The shaded area is for the stencil of the shadows. Mark them out on identical squares of stencil cardstock so that one stencil has those areas not shaded, and the other has only the shaded areas. Ensure that the two parts register perfectly before you cut them out. The stem can in fact be to the length and curvature of your choice. Otherwise, enlarge this drawing and trace off on to stencil cardstock.

Enlarge the design for the central motif shown here so that the outer circle measures 21 cm/8¼ in, the middle one 17 cm/6¾ in, and the inner one 12.5 cm/5 in. The size of the circle can, of course, be altered to suit different circumstances. The sections to be cut out are shown shaded.

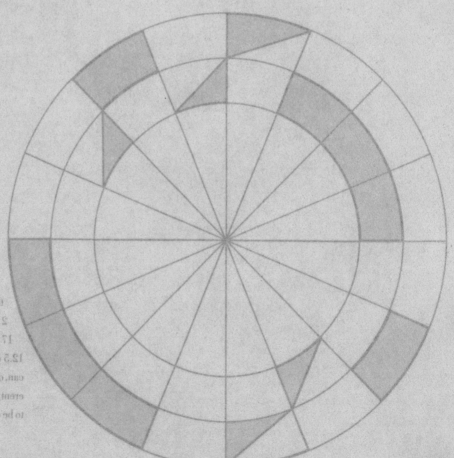

VI